Vegetarian Dash Diet Cookbook for Beginners

1000-Day Super Delicious, No-Fuss Plant-Based Recipes

with Low Sodium Meals for Losing Weight, Increasing Energy, and Lowering Blood Pressure

Darly Weller

Table of contents

Introduction

This recipe book is full of Dash diet recipes that will help curb your carb cravings. The cookbook contains vegetarian recipes divided into categories to make it easy for you. The recipes also have nutritional information to guide you on the amount of nutrients that you take into your body. And in this book, you will find a guide with all the basic information to understand what the dash diet is and the advantages it can give you.

Tasty vegetables are the must-have cookbook for anyone searching for effortless and mouth-watering recipes to satisfy your flavor. Instead of turning to options that might prevent complex, this book ensures that your body will continue to use it while still enjoying your favorite foods. With this recipe book, you will be able to make the dash diet that you won't know where to begin! The recipes in this book are quick and easy to make and will produce some wonderful meals that will become whole family favorites that you will end up making time and time again.

Chapter 1: Overview of Dash Diet

What is the Dash Diet?

Dietary Approaches to Stop Hypertension (DASH) is a type of eating plan that is specifically designed to help people prevent high blood pressure without the use of any medication.

High blood pressure or hypertension affects at least 1 billion people in the world, with low to middle-income countries having the greatest prevalence. In the United States, 45 percent of adults suffer from high blood pressure and rely heavily on medication.

High blood pressure can cause serious problems if left uncontrolled. It can overwork your heart and cause permanent damage causing a series of problems to other vital organs. Elevated blood pressures can increase your risk of heart, kidney, brain, and eye diseases, among others.

The Dash diet mainly focuses on minimizing the consumption of sodium and increasing the intake of nutrient-rich foods that can help lower blood pressure. The daily recommended consumption of sodium on a Dash diet is between 1,500 to 2,300 milligrams versus the usual consumption of 9,000 to 12,000 milligrams.

The potassium, calcium, magnesium, protein, and fiber in the food help stabilize the blood pressure, that is why foods rich in these minerals and nutrients take the center stage in the Dash diet.

Benefits of Dash Diet

Apart from keeping the blood pressure at a normal level, the Dash diet also has other wonderful health benefits in preventing diabetes, cancer, heart disease, stroke, metabolic syndrome, and other deadly diseases. The vitamins and minerals from the type of foods included in the Dash diet can balance other nutrients, improve insulin resistance, promote weight loss, and offer long-term protection against illnesses.

Since it promotes healthy eating, anybody can try and enjoy the benefits of the Dash diet even if they do not have high blood pressure. It is important to note that sodium plays an important role in the normal functioning of the body and totally eliminating it from our diets can be harmful. The Dash diet encourages a healthy balance of nutritious foods and only a reduction of our salt intake.

Foods to Eat

The Dash diet recommends eating lots of fruits and vegetables, low-fat dairy products, and whole grains. Fish, poultry, legumes, seeds, and nuts are also encouraged in moderate amounts. Highly processed foods often contain high amounts of sodium and should therefore be avoided. Likewise, sugary drinks and eating foods high in sugar are also discouraged.

Below are some examples of the foods you can eat on a Dash diet.

- Vegetables – Spinach, collard greens, kale, arugula, Swiss chard, romaine lettuce, carrot, sweet potatoes, bell peppers, and red beets.
- Fruits – Berries, banana, avocado, tomato, cantaloupe, watermelon, kiwi, and pomegranates.
- Low-fat dairy –Low-fat or skimmed milk, natural and unsweetened yogurt, mozzarella, and cottage cheese.
- Herbs and spices – Garlic, onion, ginger, black pepper, basil, rosemary, thyme, parsley, cilantro, and cinnamon.
- Lean meat and Fish – Chicken, turkey, salmon, mackerel, herring, oyster, sardine, anchovies, and seabass.

Tips for Getting Started

Each of us has different dietary requirements. If you have any existing medical conditions, don't hesitate to talk to your doctor or dietician before making big changes to your diet.

If you have been constantly experiencing high blood pressure, here are some tips you can follow to get you started with the Dash diet.

- One of the first things you can do is to know what type of foods to eat and to avoid. Your dietician can guide you with the portion sizes and the type of foods you can combine.
- Learn how to read the nutrition facts label of products to know how much sodium they contain.
- Look for unsalted versions of canned goods such as tuna, vegetables, and peas. You may also rinse them with water to wash away excess sodium.
- Opt for salt alternatives to use for cooking. Look for potassium chloride salts or sodium-free spice and herb blends as seasoning.

- Whenever possible, aim to prepare your own meals at home so you know exactly what goes into it.
- Add one serving of vegetables to at least two of your daily meals until you can eat up to five servings per day.
- Aim to get a good variety of foods to get optimum nutrients. Let vegetables take the greater portion of your meals and lean meat only as a small part.
- Frozen vegetables are a great option since you can store them longer, but make sure that you also eat fresh vegetables regularly.
- Gradually substitute refined products with whole wheat, whole oats, brown rice, buckwheat, oatmeal, and quinoa.
- Instead of snacking on crackers and sweets, eat a serving of fresh fruit when you get hungry. You may also substitute them for dessert or mix them with your unsweetened yogurt.
- Keep unsalted nuts and seeds as a snack to keep you from reaching for unhealthy foods in between meals.
- Limit your consumption of red meat and opt for protein-rich vegetables like spinach, broccoli, beans, peas, Brussels sprouts, and mushrooms.
- Use healthier oils like olive, canola, soybean, safflower, peanut, corn, almond, and sunflower when cooking or making salads.
- Try replacing some of your meals with vegetarian or vegan dishes.
- Eliminate sugary drinks, sodas, and high-sugar foods in your diet and replace them with fresh fruits and smoothies.

Chapter 2: Overview of Plant Based Diet

What Is Plant Based Diet?

A plant-based diet is not synonymous to a vegetarian or vegan diet. Although these terms are often used interchangeably, they are not the same.

A plant-based diet is focused on proportionately eating more foods primarily from plants and cutting back on animal-derived foods. However, it does not necessarily involve eliminating entire food groups and lean sources of protein. This means, those on a plant-based diet may still opt to eat some meat.

Going vegan, on the other hand, means being strictly against animal products in any form—from never eating meat and dairy products to not patronizing products tested on animals and not wearing animal products such as leather.

A healthy plant-based diet generally emphasizes meeting your nutritional needs by eating more whole plant foods, while reducing the intake of animal products. Whole foods refer to natural, unrefined or minimally refined foods. Plant foods consist of those that do not have animal ingredients such as meat, eggs, honey, milk and other dairy products.

In contrast, those on a vegetarian diet may still eat processed and refined foods. Vegetarians can even eat fast foods, junk food and other salty snacks guilt-free.

Benefits of Plant Based Diet

There are many benefits that you can enjoy once you shift to a plant-based diet.

One is that it has been proven to help ward off many serious ailments, including but not limited to the following:

- Heart disease
- High blood pressure
- Hypertension
- Type 2 diabetes
- Certain forms of cancer

Not only that, it is also said to play a role in the prevention of degenerative medical conditions such as multiple sclerosis and Alzheimer's disease.

Once you get started with this diet, you will notice a huge difference in how you feel each day. From the time that you wake up in the morning, you will feel that you have more energy, and that you do not get tired as easily as before. You will also have more mental focus and fewer mood-related problems.

As for digestion, a plant-based diet is also said to improve how the digestive system works. In fact, dieters confirm fewer incidences of stomach pains, bloating, indigestion and hyperacidity.

Then there's the weight loss benefit that we cannot forget about. Since a plant-based diet means eating fruits, vegetables, and whole grains that have fewer calories and are lower in fat, you will enjoy weight loss benefits that some other fad diets are not able to provide.

Aside from helping you lose weight; it maintains ideal weight longer because this diet is easier to sustain and does not require elimination of certain food groups.

Don't worry about not getting enough nutrients from your food intake. This diet provides all the necessary nutrients including proteins, vitamins, minerals, carbohydrates, fats, and antioxidants. And again, that's because it does not eliminate any food group but only encourages you to focus more on plant-based food products.

How Do You Start A Plant Based Diet?

Unlike with other diet programs, with the plant-based diet, you don't have to worry too much about getting stared.

As you will find out for yourself, getting started is not that difficult because most likely, you are already eating most of what is required. There's a big chance that you will only need to make minimal changes in your diet.

Here are the steps on how to get started:

Step # 1 – Write down your current diet

Do not make any changes with your diet first. For the first week, record all the dishes and snacks that you eat throughout the day. This will show you what areas in your food habits are necessary to be changed, and which ones can be retained.

Step # 2 – Write down a menu based on this diet

Once you're done with recording the past week's diet, you can now create your diet for the second week. Take note that you don't have to completely overhaul your diet immediately as this will make the transition too drastic and might not provide positive results.

Start avoiding some of the foods and drinks that are not encouraged in a plant-based diet. You should also start adding more fruits and vegetables to dishes that you love. For example, if you are fond of eating oatmeal in the morning, it would be a great idea to start packing it with bananas, apples and mangoes. If you love snacking on yogurt, make it a point to stir in some blueberries or strawberries.

Step # 3 – Cut down on meat consumption

Do not completely avoid all types of meat. But you just have to reduce intake slowly but surely. For instance, instead of eating steak with mashed potatoes on the side for dinner, why don't you try sautéing green beans with a few strips of beef and serve it with mashed potatoes on the side. This way, there are more vegetables than meat in your dish.

Step # 4 – Fill your pantry with healthy items

It's a lot harder to adopt a healthy diet if you kitchen is filled with all sorts of junk foods. Discard the candies, sweet treats, sugary beverages and bags of chips that are in your pantry. Replace these with natural and healthy snacks like kale chips, whole grain bread slices, and fruit desserts.

What to Eat

Here's a list of all the foods and drinks that you should focus on while on a plant-based diet:

- Fruits – Apples, bananas, blueberries, blackberries, pears, oranges, mangoes, avocados, pineapple, strawberries, raspberries
- Vegetables – Spinach, tomatoes, carrots, cucumber, zucchini, potatoes, squash, broccoli, cauliflower, kale, cabbage
- Whole grains – Brown rice, quinoa, oats, barley, whole wheat bread, whole wheat pasta
- Legumes – Peanuts, beans, peas, chickpeas, lentils
- Plant-based protein – Tempeh, tofu
- Nuts – Almonds, walnuts, pistachios
- Nut butters

- Seeds – Sunflower seeds, flax seeds
- Healthy oils – Olive oil, avocado oil, grapeseed oil
- Herbs and spices
- Water
- Coffee
- Tea
- Smoothies
- Fresh fruit or veggie juices

Now, here's a list of all the foods and drinks that you can consume but try to limit intake as much as possible.

- Meat – Beef, pork, lamb
- Poultry – Chicken, turkey
- Seafood – Fish, shells, crabs, shrimp
- Dairy products – Milk, cheese, yogurt
- Processed meats - Bacon, sausage

What to Avoid

This one is a list of the foods and drinks that you would want to avoid as much as possible.

- Fast food
- Sweetened beverages
- Refined grains – White bread, white rice, refined pasta
- Packaged foods – Cookies, chips, cereals

Tips

Make the transition for you easier using the following tips and strategies:

- **Make a meal planner**

Write down a menu for the week or for the month so you don't have to worry about steering away from your healthy diet. It would be a good idea to make use of an online meal planner that you can access even when you're outside your home. But if you prefer to do it the traditional way, and write it on paper, that is a good idea too.

- **Eat small healthy snacks during the day**

Doing this will keep you full longer and will reduce the possibility of getting tempted to eat foods that are not encouraged in a plant-based diet. If you are full, there's less tendency for you to crave for a huge slab of steak for instance.

- **Don't be too hard on yourself**

Making a transition from one diet to another is always difficult and challenging. Do not expect yourself to be immediately comfortable with your new diet. It may take you longer than a week. It would probably require you at least a month to ease in to your new diet, even if this is not as restrictive as other types of diet.

- **Use meat as garnish**

Instead of making it the centerpiece of your dish, use it as an "add-on". Instead of serving steak with a small number of steamed veggies on the side, it would be better to turn things around and serve more steamed veggies and just a little amount of meat.

- **Use good fats**

Make it a point to use only healthy fats like olive oil, avocados, nut butter and so on.

- **Have lots of salads**

Salads are a great way to turn your regular diet into one that's plant-based. Not only that, these are extremely convenient to prepare and will only take you a few minutes to prepare. You won't have to spend a long time in the kitchen to cook an elaborate meal.

- **Satisfy cravings for sweets with fruits**

There will always be those times when you will crave for something sweet. For some people, this usually happens after a meal. Do not deprive yourself. Instead, satisfy your craving the healthy way—eat fruits for dessert.

Follow these tips to ensure to have a smooth transition from your old diet into this new one. It may not be as challenging as with other diet programs, but of course, there will also be certain drawbacks that you would want to be prepared for.

Chapter 3: Breakfast

Date Apple Oats

Preparation Time: 10 minutes
Cooking Time: 4 minutes
Serve: 2

Ingredients:

- 1/4 cup oats
- 1/4 tsp vanilla
- 14 tsp cinnamon
- 2 dates, chopped
- 1 apple, chopped
- 1/2 cup water

Directions:

1. Spray instant pot from inside with cooking spray.
2. Add all ingredients to the instant pot and stir well.
3. Seal pot with lid and cook on high for 4 minutes.
4. Once done, allow to release pressure naturally for 10 minutes then release remaining using quick release. Remove lid.
5. Stir well and serve.

Nutritional Value (Amount per Serving):

- Calories 161
- Fat 1.1 g
- Carbohydrates 41.6 g
- Sugar 17.4 g
- Protein 2.5 g
- Cholesterol 0 mg

Simple Lemon Quinoa

Preparation Time: 10 minutes
Cooking Time: 1 minute
Serve: 4

Ingredients:

- 2 cups quinoa, rinsed and drained
- 1 fresh lemon juice
- 2 tbsp fresh parsley, chopped
- 3 cups of water
- 1/4 tsp salt

Directions:

1. Spray instant pot from inside with cooking spray.
2. Add all ingredients except lemon juice and parsley into the pot. Stir well.
3. Seal pot with lid and cook on high for 1 minute.
4. Once done, allow to release pressure naturally for 10 minutes then release remaining using quick release. Remove lid.
5. Add parsley and lemon juice.
6. Stir and serve.

Nutritional Value (Amount per Serving):

- Calories 317
- Fat 5.3 g
- Carbohydrates 54.9 g
- Sugar 0.3 g
- Protein 12.2 g
- Cholesterol 0 mg

Quinoa Breakfast Bowls

Preparation Time: 10 minutes

Cooking Time: 4 minutes

Serve: 4

Ingredients:

- 1 cup quinoa, rinsed and drained
- 1 cucumber, chopped
- 1 red bell pepper, chopped
- 1/2 cup olives, pitted and sliced
- 1 tbsp fresh basil, chopped
- 2 tbsp fresh lemon juice
- 1 tsp lemon zest, grated
- 1 1/2 cups water
- Pepper
- Salt

Directions:

1. Add quinoa, lemon zest, lemon juice, water, pepper, and salt into the instant pot and stir well.
2. Seal pot with lid and cook on high for 4 minutes.
3. Once done, allow to release pressure naturally for 10 minutes then release remaining using quick release. Remove lid.
4. Add remaining ingredients and stir well.
5. Serve immediately and enjoy it.

Nutritional Value (Amount per Serving):

- Calories 199
- Fat 4.6 g
- Carbohydrates 33.6 g
- Sugar 3 g
- Protein 7 g
- Cholesterol 0 mg

Spinach Egg Breakfast

Preparation Time: 10 minutes
Cooking Time: 8 minutes
Serve: 2

Ingredients:

- 6 eggs
- 1 tomato, chopped
- 1/2 cup mozzarella cheese, shredded
- 1 cup spinach, chopped
- 1/4 cup feta cheese, crumbled
- Pepper
- Salt

Directions:

1. Pour 1 cup of water into the instant pot then place the steamer rack in the pot.
2. In a bowl, whisk eggs with pepper and salt. Add remaining ingredients and stir well.
3. Spray heat-safe dish with cooking spray. Pour egg mixture into the prepared dish and place dish on top of the steamer rack.
4. Seal pot with lid and cook on high for 8 minutes.
5. Once done, release pressure using quick release. Remove lid.
6. Serve and enjoy.

Nutritional Value (Amount per Serving):

- Calories 267
- Fat 18.5 g
- Carbohydrates 3.8 g
- Sugar 2.7 g
- Protein 22 g
- Cholesterol 511 mg

Healthy Quinoa Rice Bowls

Preparation Time: 10 minutes

Cooking Time: 12 minutes

Serve: 4

Ingredients:

- 1/2 cup brown rice
- 1 cup quinoa
- 1/2 tsp ground cinnamon
- 1 tsp vanilla
- 1/2 tsp ground nutmeg
- 1/4 cup almonds, chopped
- 1/4 cup pecans, chopped
- 1/4 cup walnuts, chopped
- 4 cups unsweetened almond milk

Directions:

1. Spray instant pot from inside with cooking spray.
2. Add all ingredients into the instant pot and stir well.
3. Seal pot with lid and cook on high for 12 minutes.
4. Once done, allow to release pressure naturally for 5 minutes then release remaining using quick release. Remove lid.
5. Stir and serve.

Nutritional Value (Amount per Serving):

- Calories 376
- Fat 15 g
- Carbohydrates 50 g
- Sugar 0.6 g
- Protein 12 g
- Cholesterol 0 mg

Chia Carrot Oatmeal

Preparation Time: 10 minutes
Cooking Time: 10 minutes
Serve: 6

Ingredients:

- 1 cup steel-cut oats
- 1/4 cup chia seeds
- 1 cup carrot, grated
- 1 1/2 tsp ground cinnamon
- 4 cups almond milk

Directions:

1. Spray instant pot from inside with cooking spray.
2. Add all ingredients except chia seeds into the instant pot and stir well.
3. Seal pot with lid and cook on high for 10 minutes.
4. Once done, allow to release pressure naturally for 10 minutes then release remaining using quick release. Remove lid.
5. Stir in chia seeds and serve.

Nutritional Value (Amount per Serving):

- Calories 434
- Fat 39.4 g
- Carbohydrates 20.9 g
- Sugar 6.4 g
- Protein 5.8 g
- Cholesterol 0 mg

Mushroom Cheese Breakfast

Preparation Time: 10 minutes

Cooking Time: 12 minutes

Serve: 4

Ingredients:

- 5 eggs
- 2 tbsp olive oil
- 1 onion, chopped
- 2 tbsp chives, minced
- 1 1/2 cups mushrooms, sliced
- 1/2 cup almond milk
- 1/2 tbsp cheddar cheese
- 1 bell pepper, chopped
- Pepper
- Salt

Directions:

1. Add oil into the instant pot and set the pot on sauté mode.
2. Add mushrooms and sauté for 2 minutes. Transfer mushrooms on a plate and clean the instant pot.
3. In a bowl, whisk eggs with pepper and salt. Add mushrooms, onion, chives, almond milk, cheese, and bell pepper into the egg mixture and whisk well.
4. Spray baking dish with cooking spray.
5. Pour 1 1/2 cups of water into the instant pot then place steamer rack in the pot.
6. Pour egg mixture into the prepared baking dish. Cover dish with foil.
7. Place baking dish on top of the steamer rack.
8. Seal pot with lid and cook on high for 10 minutes.
9. Once done, release pressure using quick release. Remove lid.
10. Serve and enjoy.

Nutritional Value (Amount per Serving):

- Calories 238
- Fat 20.1 g
- Carbohydrates 7.9 g
- Sugar 4.6 g
- Protein 9.3 g
- Cholesterol 206 mg

Breakfast Rice Bowls

Preparation Time: 10 minutes
Cooking Time: 8 minutes
Serve: 4

Ingredients:

- 1 cup of brown rice
- 1 tsp ground cinnamon
- 1/4 cup almonds, sliced
- 2 tbsp sunflower seeds
- 1/4 cup pecans, chopped
- 1/4 cup walnuts, chopped
- 2 cup unsweetened almond milk
- Pinch of salt

Directions:

1. Spray instant pot from inside with cooking spray.
2. Add all ingredients into the instant pot and stir well.
3. Seal pot with lid and cook on high for 8 minutes.
4. Once done, allow to release pressure naturally for 5 minutes then release remaining using quick release. Remove lid.
5. Stir well and serve.

Nutritional Value (Amount per Serving):

- Calories 291
- Fat 12 g
- Carbohydrates 40.1 g
- Sugar 0.4 g
- Protein 7.6 g
- Cholesterol 0 mg

Vegetable Quinoa

Preparation Time: 10 minutes
Cooking Time: 1 minute
Serve: 6

Ingredients:

- 1 cup quinoa, rinsed and drained
- 1 1/2 cups water
- 4 cups spinach, chopped
- 1 bell pepper, chopped
- 2 carrots, chopped
- 1 celery stalk, chopped
- 1/3 cup feta cheese, crumbled
- 1/2 cup olives, sliced
- 1/3 cup pesto
- 2 tomatoes, chopped
- Pepper
- Salt

Directions:

1. Add quinoa, spinach, bell pepper, carrots, celery, water, pepper, and salt into the instant pot and stir well.
2. Seal pot with lid and cook on high for 1 minute.
3. Once done, allow to release pressure naturally for 10 minutes then release remaining using quick release. Remove lid.
4. Add remaining ingredients and stir everything well.
5. Serve and enjoy.

Nutritional Value (Amount per Serving):

- Calories 226
- Fat 10.7 g
- Carbohydrates 26 g
- Sugar 4.4 g
- Protein 7.9 g
- Cholesterol 11 mg

Pumpkin Steel Cut Oatmeal

Preparation Time: 10 minutes

Cooking Time: 10 minutes

Serve: 4

Ingredients:

- 2 cups steel-cut oats
- 1/2 cup pumpkin seeds, toasted
- 2 1/2 tbsp maple syrup
- 1 cup pumpkin puree
- 3 cups of water
- 1/4 tsp ground cinnamon
- Pinch of salt

Directions:

1. Spray instant pot from inside with cooking spray.
2. Add all ingredients except maple syrup and pumpkin seeds into the instant pot and stir well.
3. Seal pot with lid and cook on high for 10 minutes.
4. Once done, release pressure using quick release. Remove lid.
5. Add maple syrup and stir well.
6. Top with pumpkin seeds and serve.

Nutritional Value (Amount per Serving):

- Calories 302
- Fat 10.8 g
- Carbohydrates 44.2 g
- Sugar 10 g
- Protein 10.3 g
- Cholesterol 0 mg

Chapter 4: Soups & Stews

Tomato Chickpeas Stew

Preparation Time: 10 minutes
Cooking Time: 25 minutes
Serve: 4

Ingredients:

- 1 lb can chickpeas, rinsed and drained
- 18 oz can tomatoes, chopped
- 1/2 tsp red pepper flakes
- 2 tbsp olive oil
- 1 tsp dried oregano
- 1 tsp garlic, minced
- 1 onion, chopped
- Pepper
- Salt

Directions:

1. Add oil into the inner pot of instant pot and set the pot on sauté mode.
2. Add onion and garlic and sauté for 5 minutes.
3. Add remaining ingredients and stir well.
4. Seal pot with lid and cook on high pressure 20 for minutes.
5. Once done, allow to release pressure naturally for 10 minutes then release remaining using quick release. Remove lid.
6. Serve and enjoy.

Nutritional Value (Amount per Serving):

- Calories 236
- Fat 8.4 g
- Carbohydrates 35.3 g
- Sugar 5.6 g
- Protein 7.2 g
- Cholesterol 0 mg

Celery Soup

Preparation Time: 10 minutes

Cooking Time: 30 minutes

Serve: 4

Ingredients:

- 6 cups celery stalk, chopped
- 1 cup heavy cream
- 1 onion, chopped
- 2 cups vegetable broth
- 1/2 tsp dill
- Salt

Directions:

1. Add all ingredients into the instant pot and stir well.
2. Seal pot with lid and cook on high for 30 minutes.
3. Once done, release pressure using quick release. Remove lid.
4. Blend soup using an immersion blender until smooth.
5. Serve and enjoy.

Nutritional Value (Amount per Serving):

- Calories 158
- Fat 12.1 g
- Carbohydrates 8.4 g
- Sugar 3.6 g
- Protein 4.4 g
- Cholesterol 41 mg

Chicken Kale Soup

Preparation Time: 10 minutes

Cooking Time: 15 minutes

Serve: 4

Ingredients:

- 2 cups cooked chicken, chopped
- 12 oz kale, chopped
- 2 tsp garlic, minced
- 1 onion, diced
- 4 cups vegetable broth
- Salt

Directions:

1. Add all ingredients into the instant pot and stir well.
2. Seal pot with lid and cook on high for 5 minutes.
3. Once done, allow to release pressure naturally for 5 minutes then release remaining using quick release. Remove lid.
4. Stir well and serve.

Nutritional Value (Amount per Serving):

- Calories 199
- Fat 3.5 g
- Carbohydrates 12.8 g
- Sugar 1.9 g
- Protein 28.1 g
- Cholesterol 54 mg

Spinach Cauliflower Soup

Preparation Time: 10 minutes
Cooking Time: 10 minutes
Serve: 2

Ingredients:

- 1 cup cauliflower, chopped
- 3 cups spinach, chopped
- 1 tsp garlic powder
- 2 tbsp olive oil
- 3 cups vegetable broth
- 1/2 cup heavy cream
- Pepper
- Salt

Directions:

1. Add all ingredients except cream into the inner pot of instant pot and stir well.
2. Seal pot with lid and cook on high for 10 minutes.
3. Once done, release pressure using quick release. Remove lid.
4. Stir in cream and blend soup using an immersion blender until smooth.
5. Serve and enjoy.

Nutritional Value (Amount per Serving):

- Calories 309
- Fat 27.4 g
- Carbohydrates 7.5 g
- Sugar 2.8 g
- Protein 10.4 g
- Cholesterol 41 mg

Healthy Vegetable Soup

Preparation Time: 10 minutes
Cooking Time: 15 minutes
Serve: 4

Ingredients:

- 1 cup can tomatoes, chopped
- 1 small zucchini, diced
- 3 oz kale, sliced
- 1 tbsp garlic, chopped
- 5 button mushrooms, sliced
- 2 carrots, peeled and sliced
- 2 celery sticks, sliced
- 1/2 red chili, sliced
- 1 onion, diced
- 1 tbsp olive oil
- 1 bay leaf
- 4 cups vegetable stock
- 1/4 tsp salt

Directions:

1. Add oil into the inner pot of instant pot and set the pot on sauté mode.
2. Add carrots, celery, onion, and salt and cook for 2-3 minutes.
3. Add mushrooms and chili and cook for 2 minutes.
4. Add remaining ingredients and stir everything well.
5. Seal pot with lid and cook on high for 10 minutes.
6. Once done, allow to release pressure naturally for 10 minutes then release remaining using quick release. Remove lid.
7. Stir well and serve.

Nutritional Value (Amount per Serving):

- Calories 100
- Fat 3.8 g
- Carbohydrates 15.1 g
- Sugar 6.6 g
- Protein 3.5 g
- Cholesterol 0 mg

Delicious Chicken Wild Rice Soup

Preparation Time: 10 minutes

Cooking Time: 17 minutes

Serve: 4

Ingredients:

- 2 chicken breasts, boneless and cubed
- 1 tbsp fresh parsley, chopped
- 5 oz wild rice
- 28 oz chicken stock
- 1 cup carrot, chopped
- 2 tbsp olive oil
- 1 onion, chopped
- Pepper
- Salt

Directions:

1. Add oil into the inner pot of instant pot and set the pot on sauté mode.
2. Add carrot, onion, and chicken and sauté for 5 minutes.
3. Add remaining ingredients and stir well.
4. Seal pot with lid and cook on high for 12 minutes.
5. Once done, allow to release pressure naturally for 10 minutes then release remaining using quick release. Remove lid.
6. Stir well and serve.

Nutritional Value (Amount per Serving):

- Calories 356
- Fat 13.3 g
- Carbohydrates 32.5 g
- Sugar 4 g
- Protein 27.5 g
- Cholesterol 65 mg

Nutritious Kidney Bean Soup

Preparation Time: 10 minutes

Cooking Time: 1 hour 40 minutes

Serve: 8

Ingredients:

- 3 cups red kidney beans, soaked overnight & drain
- 1/4 cup fresh parsley, chopped
- 6 cups of water
- 1/4 cup olive oil
- 1 1/2 tbsp tomato paste
- 2 bell peppers, chopped
- 2 carrots, chopped
- 1 tbsp garlic, minced
- 1 onion, chopped
- 1 tsp salt

Directions:

1. Add oil into the inner pot of instant pot and set the pot on sauté mode.
2. Add garlic and onion and sauté until onion is softened.
3. Add carrots and bell peppers and sauté for 3-5 minutes.
4. Add beans, parsley, tomato paste, water, and salt and stir everything well.
5. Seal pot with lid and cook on high for 1 hour 40 minutes.
6. Once done, release pressure using quick release. Remove lid.
7. Stir well and serve.

Nutritional Value (Amount per Serving):

- Calories 312
- Fat 7.2 g
- Carbohydrates 48.4 g
- Sugar 4.7 g
- Protein 16.4 g
- Cholesterol 0 mg

Cheese Kale Soup

Preparation Time: 10 minutes
Cooking Time: 5 minutes
Serve: 4

Ingredients:

- 6 cups fresh kale, chopped
- 1 tbsp olive oil
- 3/4 cup cottage cheese, cut into chunks
- 3 cups vegetable broth
- Pepper
- salt

Directions:

1. Add all ingredients except cheese into the instant pot and stir well.
2. Seal pot with lid and cook on high for 5 minutes.
3. Once done, release pressure using quick release. Remove lid.
4. Stir in cottage cheese and serve.

Nutritional Value (Amount per Serving):

- Calories 147
- Fat 5.4 g
- Carbohydrates 12.7 g
- Sugar 0.7 g
- Protein 12.5 g
- Cholesterol 3 mg

Pepper Pumpkin Soup

Preparation Time: 10 minutes
Cooking Time: 6 minutes
Serve: 6

Ingredients:

- 2 cups pumpkin puree
- 1 onion, chopped
- 4 cups vegetable broth
- 1/4 tsp nutmeg
- 1/4 cup red bell pepper, chopped
- 1/8 tsp thyme, dried
- 1/2 tsp salt

Directions:

1. Add all ingredients into the instant pot and stir well.
2. Seal pot with lid and cook on high for 6 minutes.
3. Once done, allow to release pressure naturally for 5 minutes then release remaining using quick release. Remove lid.
4. Blend soup using an immersion blender until smooth.
5. Serve and enjoy.

Nutritional Value (Amount per Serving):

- Calories 63
- Fat 1.2 g
- Carbohydrates 9.4 g
- Sugar 4.2 g
- Protein 4.4 g
- Cholesterol 0 mg

Sausage Potato Soup

Preparation Time: 10 minutes

Cooking Time: 20 minutes

Serve: 6

Ingredients:

- 1 lb Italian sausage, crumbled
- 1 cup half and half
- 1 cup kale, chopped
- 6 cups chicken stock
- 1/2 tsp dried oregano
- 3 potatoes, peeled and diced
- 1 tsp garlic, minced
- 1 onion, chopped
- 1 tbsp olive oil
- Pepper
- Salt

Directions:

1. Add oil into the inner pot of instant pot and set the pot on sauté mode.
2. Add sausage, garlic, and onion and sauté for 5 minutes.
3. Add the rest of the ingredients and stir well.
4. Seal pot with lid and cook on high for 15 minutes.
5. Once done, allow to release pressure naturally for 10 minutes then release remaining using quick release. Remove lid.
6. Stir and serve.

Nutritional Value (Amount per Serving):

- Calories 426
- Fat 29.1 g
- Carbohydrates 22.3 g
- Sugar 2.8 g
- Protein 18.9 g
- Cholesterol 78 mg

Chapter 5: Pasta, Grains & Beans

Tasty Tomato Risotto

Preparation Time: 10 minutes
Cooking Time: 11 minutes
Serve: 2

Ingredients:

- 3/4 cup rice, rinsed and drained
- 1/2 tsp garlic powder
- 1/2 tsp cumin
- 1/3 cup tomato sauce
- 1 cup vegetable broth
- 1/2 onion, chopped
- 1 tbsp olive oil
- Salt

Directions:

1. Add oil into the inner pot of instant pot and set the pot on sauté mode.
2. Add onion and sauté for 3 minutes.
3. Add tomato sauce and broth and stir well and cook for 2 minutes.
4. Add remaining ingredients and stir well.
5. Seal pot with lid and cook on high for 6 minutes.
6. Once done, release pressure using quick release. Remove lid.
7. Stir well and serve.

Nutritional Value (Amount per Serving):

- Calories 358
- Fat 8.4 g
- Carbohydrates 61.4 g
- Sugar 3.5 g
- Protein 8.4 g
- Cholesterol 0 mg

Delicious Chicken Pasta

Preparation Time: 10 minutes

Cooking Time: 17 minutes

Serve: 4

Ingredients:

- 3 chicken breasts, skinless, boneless, cut into pieces
- 9 oz whole-grain pasta
- 1/2 cup olives, sliced
- 1/2 cup sun-dried tomatoes
- 1 tbsp roasted red peppers, chopped
- 14 oz can tomatoes, diced
- 2 cups marinara sauce
- 1 cup chicken broth
- Pepper
- Salt

Directions:

1. Add all ingredients except whole-grain pasta into the instant pot and stir well.
2. Seal pot with lid and cook on high for 12 minutes.
3. Once done, allow to release pressure naturally. Remove lid.
4. Add pasta and stir well. Seal pot again and select manual and set timer for 5 minutes.
5. Once done, allow to release pressure naturally for 5 minutes then release remaining using quick release. Remove lid.
6. Stir well and serve.

Nutritional Value (Amount per Serving):

- Calories 615
- Fat 15.4 g
- Carbohydrates 71 g
- Sugar 17.6 g
- Protein 48 g
- Cholesterol 100 mg

Tasty Salsa Beans

Preparation Time: 10 minutes
Cooking Time: 40 minutes
Serve: 6

Ingredients:

- 20 oz package ham pinto beans, rinsed
- 1 jalapeno pepper, diced
- 1 onion, diced
- 5 cups vegetable broth
- 1/4 cup parsley, chopped
- 1/2 cup salsa
- 1/2 tsp garlic, chopped
- Pepper
- Salt

Directions:

1. Add all ingredients into the inner pot of instant pot and stir well.
2. Seal pot with lid and cook on high for 40 minutes.
3. Once done, allow to release pressure naturally. Remove lid.
4. Stir well and serve.

Nutritional Value (Amount per Serving):

- Calories 147
- Fat 2.3 g
- Carbohydrates 27.6 g
- Sugar 2.1 g
- Protein 12.5 g
- Cholesterol 0 mg

Corn Risotto

Preparation Time: 10 minutes
Cooking Time: 12 minutes
Serve: 4

Ingredients:

- 1 cup of rice
- 3 cups vegetable broth
- 1 tbsp olive oil
- 1 tsp garlic, minced
- 1 onion, chopped
- 3/4 cup sweet corn
- 1 red pepper, diced
- 1 tsp dried mix herbs
- 1/4 tsp pepper
- 1/2 tsp salt

Directions:

1. Add oil into the inner pot of instant pot and set the pot on sauté mode.
2. Add onion and garlic and sauté for 5 minutes.
3. Add the rest of the ingredients and stir well.
4. Seal pot with lid and cook on high for 8 minutes.
5. Once done, release pressure using quick release. Remove lid.
6. Stir well and serve.

Nutritional Value (Amount per Serving):

- Calories 304
- Fat 5.3 g
- Carbohydrates 54.5 g
- Sugar 4.7 g
- Protein 9.5 g
- Cholesterol 0 mg

Healthy Spinach Rice

Preparation Time: 10 minutes
Cooking Time: 16 minutes
Serve: 4

Ingredients:

- 1 1/2 cups rice
- 2 tbsp fresh lemon juice
- 3 1/2 cups vegetable stock
- 12 oz spinach, chopped
- 1/2 cup onion, chopped
- 2 tbsp olive oil
- 1 tsp garlic, minced
- Pepper
- Salt

Directions:

1. Add oil into the inner pot of instant pot and set the pot on sauté mode.
2. Add onion and garlic and sauté for 5 minutes.
3. Add remaining ingredients except spinach and stir well.
4. Seal pot with lid and cook on high for 8 minutes.
5. Once done, allow to release pressure naturally for 5 minutes then release remaining using quick release. Remove lid.
6. Add spinach and stir well and cook on sauté mode for 3 minutes.
7. Serve and enjoy.

Nutritional Value (Amount per Serving):

- Calories 347
- Fat 8 g
- Carbohydrates 61.1 g
- Sugar 1.8 g
- Protein 8 g
- Cholesterol 0 mg

Brown Rice Pilaf

Preparation Time: 10 minutes
Cooking Time: 27 minutes
Serve: 6

Ingredients:

- 1 1/2 cups brown rice, rinsed and drained
- 2 tbsp parsley, chopped
- 1 3/4 cups vegetable broth
- 1 tsp garlic, minced
- 1/2 cup onion, diced
- 2 tbsp olive oil
- 1/2 tsp salt

Directions:

1. Add oil into the inner pot of instant pot and set the pot on sauté mode.
2. Add onion and sauté for 5 minutes.
3. Add the rest of the ingredients except parsley and stir well.
4. Seal pot with lid and cook on high for 22 minutes.
5. Once done, allow to release pressure naturally. Remove lid.
6. Garnish with parsley and serve.

Nutritional Value (Amount per Serving):

- Calories 228
- Fat 6.4 g
- Carbohydrates 37.6 g
- Sugar 0.6 g
- Protein 5.2 g
- Cholesterol 0 mg

Quick & Easy Couscous

Preparation Time: 10 minutes
Cooking Time: 5 minutes
Serve: 4

Ingredients:

- 2 cups couscous
- 2 tbsp fresh parsley, chopped
- 2 1/2 cups vegetable stock
- Pepper
- Salt

Directions:

1. Add couscous and vegetable stock into the instant pot.
2. Seal pot with lid and cook on high for 5 minutes.
3. Once done, allow to release pressure naturally for 10 minutes then release remaining using quick release. Remove lid.
4. Stir in remaining ingredients and serve.

Nutritional Value (Amount per Serving):

- Calories 330
- Fat 0.6 g
- Carbohydrates 67.7 g
- Sugar 0.5 g
- Protein 11.4 g
- Cholesterol 0 mg

Leek Rice Pilaf

Preparation Time: 10 minutes
Cooking Time: 20 minutes
Serve: 4

Ingredients:

- 1 1/2 cups rice
- 2 tsp ground cumin
- 2 tbsp fresh parsley, chopped
- 3 cups vegetable stock
- 1 tsp chili powder
- 2 leeks, chopped
- 2 tbsp olive oil
- 1 tsp garlic, minced
- Pepper
- Salt

Directions:

1. Add oil into the inner pot of instant pot and set the pot on sauté mode.
2. Add leek and garlic and sauté for 2 minutes.
3. Add remaining ingredients and stir well.
4. Seal pot with lid and cook on high for 18 minutes.
5. Once done, allow to release pressure naturally for 10 minutes then release remaining using quick release. Remove lid.
6. Serve and enjoy.

Nutritional Value (Amount per Serving):

- Calories 353
- Fat 8 g
- Carbohydrates 63.6 g
- Sugar 2.5 g
- Protein 6.3 g
- Cholesterol 0 mg

Flavors Taco Rice Bowl

Preparation Time: 10 minutes

Cooking Time: 14 minutes

Serve: 8

Ingredients:

- 1 lb ground beef
- 8 oz cheddar cheese, shredded
- 14 oz can red beans
- 2 oz taco seasoning
- 16 oz salsa
- 2 cups of water
- 2 cups brown rice
- Pepper
- Salt

Directions:

1. Set instant pot on sauté mode.
2. Add meat to the pot and sauté until brown.
3. Add water, beans, rice, taco seasoning, pepper, and salt and stir well.
4. Top with salsa. Seal pot with lid and cook on high for 14 minutes.
5. Once done, release pressure using quick release. Remove lid.
6. Add cheddar cheese and stir until cheese is melted.
7. Serve and enjoy.

Nutritional Value (Amount per Serving):

- Calories 464
- Fat 15.3 g
- Carbohydrates 48.9 g
- Sugar 2.8 g
- Protein 32.2 g
- Cholesterol 83 mg

Lentil Rice

Preparation Time: 10 minutes
Cooking Time: 20 minutes
Serve: 6

Ingredients:

- 1 1/2 cups brown rice
- 1/2 cup dry green lentils
- 3 1/2 cups vegetable stock
- 2 tbsp olive oil
- 1 tsp sea salt

Directions:

1. Add oil into the inner pot of instant pot and set the pot on sauté mode.
2. Add rice and sauté for 5 minutes.
3. Add remaining ingredients and stir well.
4. Seal pot with lid and cook on high for 15 minutes.
5. Once done, allow to release pressure naturally for 10 minutes then release remaining using quick release. Remove lid.
6. Serve and enjoy.

Nutritional Value (Amount per Serving):

- Calories 272
- Fat 6.2 g
- Carbohydrates 46.3 g
- Sugar 0.7 g
- Protein 7.9 g
- Cholesterol 0 mg

Chapter 6: lunch

Easy Curried Spinach Chickpeas

Preparation Time: 10 minutes

Cooking Time: 35 minutes

Serve: 6

Ingredients:

- 1 cup dry chickpeas, rinsed
- 2 cups spinach, chopped
- 1/8 tsp ground nutmeg
- 1 tbsp curry powder
- 1/2 tsp garlic powder
- 14 oz can tomatoes, crushed
- 4 cup vegetable stock
- Pepper
- Salt

Directions:

1. Add chickpeas and stock into the instant pot.
2. Seal pot with lid and cook on high for 30 minutes.
3. Once done, allow to release pressure naturally for 10 minutes then release remaining using quick release. Remove lid.
4. Drain excess liquid from chickpeas. Set pot on sauté mode.
5. Add remaining ingredients and stir well and cook for 5 minutes.
6. Stir well and serve.

Nutritional Value (Amount per Serving):

- Calories 146
- Fat 2.3 g
- Carbohydrates 25.4 g
- Sugar 6.4 g
- Protein 7.8 g
- Cholesterol 0 mg

Tomato & Cheese Mix

Preparation Time: 10 minutes
Cooking Time: 15 minutes
Serve: 4

Ingredients:

- 1 lb grape tomatoes, halved
- 1 cup feta cheese, crumbled
- 1 cup heavy cream
- 1 onion, chopped
- 1 tbsp olive oil
- 1/4 tsp Italian seasoning
- Pepper
- Salt

Directions:

1. Add oil into the inner pot of instant pot and set the pot on sauté mode.
2. Add onion and sauté for 3 minutes.
3. Add remaining ingredients and stir well.
4. Seal pot with lid and cook on high for 12 minutes.
5. Once done, release pressure using quick release. Remove lid.
6. Stir and serve.

Nutritional Value (Amount per Serving):

- Calories 265
- Fat 22.9 g
- Carbohydrates 9.4 g
- Sugar 5.7 g
- Protein 7.3 g
- Cholesterol 75 mg

Tomato Dill Cauliflower

Preparation Time: 10 minutes

Cooking Time: 12 minutes

Serve: 4

Ingredients:

- 1 lb cauliflower florets, chopped
- 1 tbsp fresh dill, chopped
- 1/4 tsp Italian seasoning
- 1 tbsp vinegar
- 1 cup can tomatoes, crushed
- 1 cup vegetable stock
- 1 tsp garlic, minced
- Pepper
- Salt

Directions:

1. Add all ingredients except dill into the instant pot and stir well.
2. Seal pot with lid and cook on high for 12 minutes.
3. Once done, allow to release pressure naturally for 10 minutes then release remaining using quick release. Remove lid.
4. Garnish with dill and serve.

Nutritional Value (Amount per Serving):

- Calories 47
- Fat 0.3 g
- Carbohydrates 10 g
- Sugar 5 g
- Protein 3.1 g
- Cholesterol 0 mg

Creamy Lemon Bell Peppers

Preparation Time: 10 minutes
Cooking Time: 15 minutes
Serve: 4

Ingredients:

- 1 lb bell peppers, cut into strips
- 1 tbsp chives, chopped
- 1 tbsp fresh lime juice
- 1/2 cup heavy cream
- 1/4 tsp dried mix herbs
- Pepper
- Salt

Directions:

1. Add all ingredients into the inner pot of instant pot and stir well.
2. Seal pot with lid and cook on high for 15 minutes.
3. Once done, allow to release pressure naturally for 5 minutes then release remaining using quick release. Remove lid.
4. Stir and serve.

Nutritional Value (Amount per Serving):

- Calories 72
- Fat 5.7 g
- Carbohydrates 5.2 g
- Sugar 1.8 g
- Protein 0.9 g
- Cholesterol 21 mg

Healthy Vegetable Medley

Preparation Time: 10 minutes
Cooking Time: 17 minutes
Serve: 6

Ingredients:

- 3 cups broccoli florets
- 1 sweet potato, chopped
- 1 tsp garlic, minced
- 14 oz coconut milk
- 28 oz can tomatoes, chopped
- 14 oz can chickpeas, drained and rinsed
- 1 onion, chopped
- 1 tbsp olive oil
- 1 tsp Italian seasoning
- Pepper
- Salt

Directions:

1. Add oil into the inner pot of instant pot and set the pot on sauté mode.
2. Add garlic and onion and sauté until onion is softened.
3. Add remaining ingredients and stir everything well.
4. Seal pot with lid and cook on high for 12 minutes.
5. Once done, allow to release pressure naturally for 10 minutes then release remaining using quick release. Remove lid.
6. Stir well and serve.

Nutritional Value (Amount per Serving):

- Calories 322
- Fat 19.3 g
- Carbohydrates 34.3 g
- Sugar 9.6 g
- Protein 7.9 g
- Cholesterol 1 mg

Easy Chili Pepper Zucchinis

Preparation Time: 10 minutes
Cooking Time: 10 minutes
Serve: 4

Ingredients:

- 4 zucchinis, cut into cubes
- 1/2 tsp red pepper flakes
- 1/2 tsp cayenne
- 1 tbsp chili powder
- 1/4 cup vegetable stock
- Salt

Directions:

1. Add all ingredients into the inner pot of instant pot and stir well.
2. Seal pot with lid and cook on high for 10 minutes.
3. Once done, allow to release pressure naturally for 10 minutes then release remaining using quick release. Remove lid.
4. Stir and serve.

Nutritional Value (Amount per Serving):

- Calories 38
- Fat 0.7 g
- Carbohydrates 8.8 g
- Sugar 3.6 g
- Protein 2.7 g
- Cholesterol 0 mg

Spicy Cauliflower

Preparation Time: 10 minutes

Cooking Time: 6 minutes

Serve: 2

Ingredients:

- 1/2 small cauliflower head, cut into florets
- 1 tbsp fresh parsley, chopped
- 1/2 cup water
- 1/4 tsp paprika
- 1/4 tsp turmeric
- 1/2 tsp ground cumin
- 1 tbsp olive oil
- 1/4 tsp chili powder
- 1/4 small onion, chopped
- 1 tomato, chopped
- Pepper
- Salt

Directions:

1. Add tomato, onion, and chili powder into the blender and blend until smooth.
2. Add oil into the inner pot of instant pot and set the pot on sauté mode.
3. Add blended tomato mixture into the pot and cook for 2-3 minutes.
4. Add paprika, cumin, turmeric, and pepper and stir for a minute.
5. Add remaining ingredients and stir well.
6. Seal pot with lid and cook on high for 3 minutes.
7. Once done, release pressure using quick release. Remove lid.
8. Stir and serve.

Nutritional Value (Amount per Serving):

- Calories 97
- Fat 7.5 g
- Carbohydrates 7.6 g
- Sugar 3.7 g
- Protein 2.2 g
- Cholesterol 0 mg

Zesty Green Beans

Preparation Time: 10 minutes
Cooking Time: 15 minutes
Serve: 4

Ingredients:

- 1 lb green beans, trimmed
- 1 cup vegetable stock
- 1 lemon juice
- 1 tsp lemon zest, grated
- Pepper
- Salt

Directions:

1. Pour the stock into the instant pot.
2. Add green beans, lemon juice, lemon zest, pepper, and salt into the bowl and toss well.
3. Transfer green beans into the steamer basket. Place a steamer basket in the pot.
4. Seal pot with lid and cook on high for 15 minutes.
5. Once done, allow to release pressure naturally for 5 minutes then release remaining using quick release. Remove lid.
6. Serve and enjoy.

Nutritional Value (Amount per Serving):

- Calories 40
- Fat 0.3 g
- Carbohydrates 8.7 g
- Sugar 2.1 g
- Protein 2.3 g
- Cholesterol 0 mg

Potato Salad

Preparation Time: 10 minutes
Cooking Time: 10 minutes
Serve: 8

Ingredients:

- 5 cups potato, cubed
- 1/4 cup fresh parsley, chopped
- 1/4 tsp red pepper flakes
- 1 tbsp olive oil
- 1/3 cup mayonnaise
- 1/2 tbsp oregano
- 2 tbsp capers
- 3/4 cup feta cheese, crumbled
- 1 cup olives, halved
- 3 cups of water
- 3/4 cup onion, chopped
- Pepper
- Salt

Directions:

1. Add potatoes, onion, and salt into the instant pot.
2. Seal pot with lid and cook on high for 3 minutes.
3. Once done, release pressure using quick release. Remove lid.
4. Remove potatoes from pot and place in a large mixing bowl.
5. Add remaining ingredients and stir everything well.
6. Serve and enjoy.

Nutritional Value (Amount per Serving):

- Calories 152
- Fat 9.9 g
- Carbohydrates 13.6 g
- Sugar 2.1 g
- Protein 3.5 g
- Cholesterol 15 mg

Creamy Dill Potatoes

Preparation Time: 10 minutes
Cooking Time: 20 minutes
Serve: 4

Ingredients:

- 2 lbs potatoes, peeled and cut into chunks
- 1 tbsp fresh dill, chopped
- 1 cup vegetable stock
- 3/4 cup heavy cream
- Pepper
- Salt

Directions:

1. Add all ingredients into the inner pot of instant pot and stir well.
2. Seal pot with lid and cook on high for 20 minutes.
3. Once done, allow to release pressure naturally for 10 minutes then release remaining using quick release. Remove lid.
4. Stir and serve.

Nutritional Value (Amount per Serving):

- Calories 238
- Fat 8.6 g
- Carbohydrates 37 g
- Sugar 2.8 g
- Protein 4.5 g
- Cholesterol 31 mg

Chapter 7: Appetizers

Creamy Potato Spread

Preparation Time: 10 minutes
Cooking Time: 15 minutes
Serve: 6

Ingredients:

- 1 lb sweet potatoes, peeled and chopped
- 3/4 tbsp fresh chives, chopped
- 1/2 tsp paprika
- 1 tbsp garlic, minced
- 1 cup tomato puree
- Pepper
- Salt

Directions:

1. Add all ingredients except chives into the inner pot of instant pot and stir well.
2. Seal pot with lid and cook on high for 15 minutes.
3. Once done, allow to release pressure naturally for 10 minutes then release remaining using quick release. Remove lid.
4. Transfer instant pot sweet potato mixture into the food processor and process until smooth.
5. Garnish with chives and serve.

Nutritional Value (Amount per Serving):

- Calories 108
- Fat 0.3 g
- Carbohydrates 25.4 g
- Sugar 2.4 g
- Protein 2 g
- Cholesterol 0 mg

Spicy Pepper Eggplant Spread

Preparation Time: 10 minutes

Cooking Time: 9 minutes

Serve: 4

Ingredients:

- 3 cups Italian eggplants, cut into 1/-inch chunks
- 1/2 cup tomatoes, diced
- 1 cup red pepper, diced
- 1/2 tsp red pepper flakes
- 1 tbsp vinegar
- 2 tbsp garlic, minced
- 1/2 cup onion, diced
- 2 tbsp olive oil
- 1/4 cup water
- 1 tsp kosher salt

Directions:

1. Add oil into the inner pot of instant pot and set the pot on sauté mode.
2. Add red pepper and eggplant and sauté for 5 minutes.
3. Add remaining ingredients and stir everything well.
4. Seal pot with lid and cook on high for 4 minutes.
5. Once done, release pressure using quick release. Remove lid.
6. Mash the spread mixture using the spatula and serve.

Nutritional Value (Amount per Serving):

- Calories 237
- Fat 19.2 g
- Carbohydrates 18 g
- Sugar 2.8 g
- Protein 1 g
- Cholesterol 0 mg

Olive Eggplant Spread

Preparation Time: 10 minutes

Cooking Time: 8 minutes

Serve: 12

Ingredients:

- 1 3/4 lbs eggplant, chopped
- 1/2 tbsp dried oregano
- 1/4 cup olives, pitted and chopped
- 1 tbsp tahini
- 1/4 cup fresh lime juice
- 1/2 cup water
- 2 garlic cloves
- 1/4 cup olive oil
- Salt

Directions:

1. Add oil into the inner pot of instant pot and set the pot on sauté mode.
2. Add eggplant and cook for 3-5 minutes. Turn off sauté mode.
3. Add water and salt and stir well.
4. Seal pot with lid and cook on high for 3 minutes.
5. Once done, release pressure using quick release. Remove lid.
6. Drain eggplant well and transfer into the food processor.
7. Add remaining ingredients into the food processor and process until smooth.
8. Serve and enjoy.

Nutritional Value (Amount per Serving):

- Calories 65
- Fat 5.3 g
- Carbohydrates 4.7 g
- Sugar 2 g
- Protein 0.9 g
- Cholesterol 0 mg

Pepper Tomato Eggplant Spread

Preparation Time: 10 minutes
Cooking Time: 10 minutes
Serve: 3

Ingredients:

- 2 cups eggplant, chopped
- 1/4 cup vegetable broth
- 2 tbsp tomato paste
- 1/4 cup sun-dried tomatoes, minced
- 1 cup bell pepper, chopped
- 1 tsp garlic, minced
- 1 cup onion, chopped
- 3 tbsp olive oil
- Salt

Directions:

1. Add oil into the inner pot of instant pot and set the pot on sauté mode.
2. Add onion and sauté for 3 minutes.
3. Add eggplant, bell pepper, and garlic and sauté for 2 minutes.
4. Add remaining ingredients and stir well.
5. Seal pot with lid and cook on high for 5 minutes.
6. Once done, release pressure using quick release. Remove lid.
7. Lightly mash the eggplant mixture using a potato masher.
8. Stir well and serve.

Nutritional Value (Amount per Serving):

- Calories 178
- Fat 14.4 g
- Carbohydrates 12.8 g
- Sugar 7 g
- Protein 2.4 g
- Cholesterol 0 mg

Balsamic Bell Pepper Salsa

Preparation Time: 10 minutes

Cooking Time: 6 minutes

Serve: 2

Ingredients:

- 2 red bell peppers, chopped and seeds removed
- 1 cup grape tomatoes, halved
- 1/2 tbsp cayenne
- 1 tbsp balsamic vinegar
- 2 cup vegetable broth
- 1/2 cup sour cream
- 1/2 tsp garlic powder
- 1/2 onion, chopped
- Salt

Directions:

1. Add all ingredients except cream into the instant pot and stir well.
2. Seal pot with lid and cook on high for 6 minutes.
3. Once done, release pressure using quick release. Remove lid.
4. Add sour cream and stir well.
5. Blend the salsa mixture using an immersion blender until smooth.
6. Serve and enjoy.

Nutritional Value (Amount per Serving):

- Calories 235
- Fat 14.2 g
- Carbohydrates 19.8 g
- Sugar 10.7 g
- Protein 9.2 g
- Cholesterol 25 mg

Spicy Chicken Dip

Preparation Time: 10 minutes
Cooking Time: 15 minutes
Serve: 10

Ingredients:

- 1 lb chicken breast, skinless and boneless
- 1/2 cup sour cream
- 8 oz cheddar cheese, shredded
- 1/2 cup chicken stock
- 2 jalapeno pepper, sliced
- 8 oz cream cheese
- Pepper
- Salt

Directions:

1. Add chicken, stock, jalapenos, and cream cheese into the instant pot.
2. Seal pot with lid and cook on high for 12 minutes.
3. Once done, release pressure using quick release. Remove lid.
4. Shred chicken using a fork.
5. Set pot on sauté mode. Add remaining ingredients and stir well and cook until cheese is melted.
6. Serve and enjoy.

Nutritional Value (Amount per Serving):

- Calories 248
- Fat 19 g
- Carbohydrates 1.6 g
- Sugar 0.3 g
- Protein 17.4 g
- Cholesterol 83 mg

Pinto Bean Dip

Preparation Time: 10 minutes
Cooking Time: 45 minutes
Serve: 6

Ingredients:

- 1 cup dry pinto beans
- 2 tsp chili powder
- 3 chilies de Arbol, remove the stem
- 4 cups of water
- 1 tsp salt

Directions:

1. Add beans, chilies, and water into the instant pot and stir well.
2. Seal pot with lid and cook on high for 45 minutes.
3. Once done, allow to release pressure naturally for 10 minutes then release remaining using quick release. Remove lid.
4. Transfer instant pot bean mixture into the blender along with chili powder and salt and blend until smooth.
5. Serve and enjoy.

Nutritional Value (Amount per Serving):

- Calories 139
- Fat 0.6 g
- Carbohydrates 24.6 g
- Sugar 4.2 g
- Protein 8 g
- Cholesterol 0 mg

Spicy Jalapeno Spinach Artichoke Dip

Preparation Time: 10 minutes
Cooking Time: 3 minutes
Serve: 15

Ingredients:

- 10 oz spinach, chopped
- 1/2 cup parmesan cheese, grated
- 8 oz Italian cheese, shredded
- 1/4 cup fresh parsley, chopped
- 2 tbsp jalapeno, diced
- 1 1/2 tbsp garlic, minced
- 2 tbsp green onion, chopped
- 14 oz cream cheese, cubed
- 18 oz jar marinated artichoke hearts, chopped
- 1 1/2 tbsp fresh lemon juice
- 1/2 cup vegetable stock

Directions:

1. Add all ingredients except parmesan cheese and Italian cheese into the instant pot and stir well.
2. Seal pot with lid and cook on high for 3 minutes.
3. Once done, allow to release pressure naturally for 5 minutes then release remaining using quick release. Remove lid.
4. Set pot on sauté mode. Add parmesan cheese and Italian cheese and stir well and cook until cheese is melted.
5. Serve and enjoy.

Nutritional Value (Amount per Serving):

- Calories 195
- Fat 16.3 g
- Carbohydrates 3.7 g
- Sugar 0.6 g
- Protein 6.7 g
- Cholesterol 42 mg

Tomato Olive Salsa

Preparation Time: 10 minutes

Cooking Time: 5 minutes

Serve: 4

Ingredients:

- 2 cups olives, pitted and chopped
- 1/4 cup fresh parsley, chopped
- 1/4 cup fresh basil, chopped
- 2 tbsp green onion, chopped
- 1 cup grape tomatoes, halved
- 1 tbsp olive oil
- 1 tbsp vinegar
- Pepper
- Salt

Directions:

1. Add all ingredients into the inner pot of instant pot and stir well.
2. Seal pot with lid and cook on high for 5 minutes.
3. Once done, allow to release pressure naturally for 5 minutes then release remaining using quick release. Remove lid.
4. Stir well and serve.

Nutritional Value (Amount per Serving):

- Calories 119
- Fat 10.8 g
- Carbohydrates 6.5 g
- Sugar 1.3 g
- Protein 1.2 g
- Cholesterol 0 mg

Rosemary Cauliflower Dip

Preparation Time: 10 minutes

Cooking Time: 15 minutes

Serve: 4

Ingredients:

- 1 lb cauliflower florets
- 1 tbsp fresh parsley, chopped
- 1/2 cup heavy cream
- 1/2 cup vegetable stock
- 1 tbsp garlic, minced
- 1 tbsp rosemary, chopped
- 1 tbsp olive oil
- 1 onion, chopped
- Pepper
- Salt

Directions:

1. Add oil into the inner pot of instant pot and set the pot on sauté mode.
2. Add onion and sauté for 5 minutes.
3. Add remaining ingredients except for parsley and heavy cream and stir well.
4. Seal pot with lid and cook on high for 10 minutes.
5. Once done, allow to release pressure naturally for 10 minutes then release remaining using quick release. Remove lid.
6. Add cream and stir well. Blend cauliflower mixture using immersion blender until smooth.
7. Garnish with parsley and serve.

Nutritional Value (Amount per Serving):

- Calories 128
- Fat 9.4 g
- Carbohydrates 10.4 g
- Sugar 4 g
- Protein 3.1 g
- Cholesterol 21 mg

Chapter 8: Desserts

Creamy Fruit Bowls

Preparation Time: 10 minutes
Cooking Time: 1 minute
Serve: 4

Ingredients:

- 1 cup heavy cream
- 1 cup grapes, halved
- 1 avocado, peeled and cubed
- 3 cups pineapple, peeled and cubed
- 1 cup mango, peeled and cubed
- 1/2 tsp vanilla

Directions:

1. Add mango, pineapple, avocado, and grapes into the instant pot and stir well.
2. Seal pot with lid and cook on high for 1 minute.
3. Once done, release pressure using quick release. Remove lid.
4. Stir in vanilla and heavy cream.
5. Serve and enjoy.

Nutritional Value (Amount per Serving):

- Calories 309
- Fat 21.3 g
- Carbohydrates 31.6 g
- Sugar 21.9 g
- Protein 2.7 g
- Cholesterol 41 mg

Healthy Zucchini Pudding

Preparation Time: 10 minutes
Cooking Time: 10 minutes
Serve: 4

Ingredients:

- 2 cups zucchini, shredded
- 1/4 tsp cardamom powder
- 5 oz half and half
- 5 oz almond milk
- 1/4 cup Swerve

Directions:

1. Add all ingredients except cardamom into the instant pot and stir well.
2. Seal pot with lid and cook on high for 10 minutes.
3. Once done, allow to release pressure naturally for 10 minutes then release remaining using quick release. Remove lid.
4. Stir in cardamom and serve.

Nutritional Value (Amount per Serving):

- Calories 137
- Fat 12.6 g
- Carbohydrates 20.5 g
- Sugar 17.2 g
- Protein 2.6 g
- Cholesterol 13 mg

Fruit Nut Bowl

Preparation Time: 10 minutes
Cooking Time: 10 minutes
Serve: 2

Ingredients:

- 1/4 cup pecans, chopped
- 1/4 cup shredded coconut
- 1 cup of water
- 3 tbsp coconut oil
- 1/2 tsp cinnamon
- 1 pear, chopped
- 1 plum, chopped
- 2 tbsp Swerve
- 1 apple, chopped

Directions:

1. In a heat-safe dish add coconut, coconut oil, pear, apple, plum, and swerve and mix well.
2. Pour water into the instant pot then place the trivet in the pot.
3. Place dish on top of the trivet.
4. Seal pot with lid and cook on high for 10 minutes.
5. Once done, release pressure using quick release. Remove lid.
6. Remove dish from pot carefully. Top with pecans and serve.

Nutritional Value (Amount per Serving):

- Calories 338
- Fat 25.4 g
- Carbohydrates 47.2 g
- Sugar 37.6 g
- Protein 1.4 g
- Cholesterol 0 mg

Chunky Apple Sauce

Preparation Time: 10 minutes
Cooking Time: 12 minutes
Serve: 16

Ingredients:

- 4 apples, peeled, cored and diced
- 1 tsp vanilla
- 4 pears, diced
- 2 tbsp cinnamon
- 1/4 cup maple syrup
- 3/4 cup water

Directions:

1. Add all ingredients into the instant pot and stir well.
2. Seal pot with lid and cook on high for 12 minutes.
3. Once done, allow to release pressure naturally for 10 minutes then release remaining using quick release. Remove lid.
4. Serve and enjoy.

Nutritional Value (Amount per Serving):

- Calories 75
- Fat 0.2 g
- Carbohydrates 19.7 g
- Sugar 13.9 g
- Protein 0.4 g
- Cholesterol 0 mg

Coconut Risotto Pudding

Preparation Time: 10 minutes
Cooking Time: 20 minutes
Serve: 6

Ingredients:

- 3/4 cup rice
- 1/2 cup shredded coconut
- 1 tsp lemon juice
- 1/2 tsp vanilla
- 14.5 oz can coconut milk
- 1/4 cup maple syrup
- 1 1/2 cups water

Directions:

1. Add all ingredients into the instant pot and stir well.
2. Seal pot with lid and cook on high for 20 minutes.
3. Once done, allow to release pressure naturally for 10 minutes then release remaining using quick release. Remove lid.
4. Blend pudding mixture using an immersion blender until smooth.
5. Serve and enjoy.

Nutritional Value (Amount per Serving):

- Calories 205
- Fat 8.6 g
- Carbohydrates 29.1 g
- Sugar 9 g
- Protein 2.6 g
- Cholesterol 0 mg

Apple Orange Stew

Preparation Time: 10 minutes
Cooking Time: 10 minutes
Serve: 4

Ingredients:

- 4 apples, cored and cut into wedges
- 1 tsp liquid stevia
- 1/2 cup orange juice
- 1 cup apple juice
- 1 tsp vanilla

Directions:

1. Add all ingredients into the inner pot of instant pot and stir well.
2. Seal pot with lid and cook on high for 10 minutes.
3. Once done, allow to release pressure naturally for 10 minutes then release remaining using quick release. Remove lid.
4. Stir well and serve.

Nutritional Value (Amount per Serving):

- Calories 161
- Fat 0.5 g
- Carbohydrates 41.2 g
- Sugar 31.9 g
- Protein 0.9 g
- Cholesterol 0 mg

Pear Sauce

Preparation Time: 10 minutes
Cooking Time: 15 minutes
Serve: 6

Ingredients:

- 10 pears, sliced
- 1 cup apple juice
- 1 1/2 tsp cinnamon
- 1/4 tsp nutmeg

Directions:

1. Add all ingredients into the instant pot and stir well.
2. Seal pot with lid and cook on high for 15 minutes.
3. Once done, allow to release pressure naturally for 10 minutes then release remaining using quick release. Remove lid.
4. Blend the pear mixture using an immersion blender until smooth.
5. Serve and enjoy.

Nutritional Value (Amount per Serving):

- Calories 222
- Fat 0.6 g
- Carbohydrates 58.2 g
- Sugar 38 g
- Protein 1.3 g
- Cholesterol 0 mg

Apple Dates Mix

Preparation Time: 10 minutes

Cooking Time: 15 minutes

Serve: 4

Ingredients:

- 4 apples, cored and cut into chunks
- 1 tsp vanilla
- 1 tsp cinnamon
- 1/2 cup dates, pitted
- 1 1/2 cups apple juice

Directions:

1. Add all ingredients into the inner pot of instant pot and stir well.
2. Seal pot with lid and cook on high for 15 minutes.
3. Once done, allow to release pressure naturally for 10 minutes then release remaining using quick release. Remove lid.
4. Stir and serve.

Nutritional Value (Amount per Serving):

- Calories 226
- Fat 0.6 g
- Carbohydrates 58.6 g
- Sugar 46.4 g
- Protein 1.3 g
- Cholesterol 0 mg

Creamy Brown Rice Pudding

Preparation Time: 10 minutes
Cooking Time: 20 minutes
Serve: 8

Ingredients:

- 1 cup of rice
- 1 cup of brown rice
- 1 cup of water
- 1 cup half and half
- 1/2 cup pecans, chopped
- 2 tsp vanilla
- 1 tbsp coconut butter
- 1/2 cup heavy cream
- Pinch of salt

Directions:

1. Add coconut butter into the instant pot and set the pot on sauté mode.
2. Add pecans into the pot and stir until toasted.
3. Add remaining ingredients except for heavy cream and vanilla. Stir well.
4. Seal pot with lid and cook on high for 20 minutes.
5. Once done, allow to release pressure naturally for 10 minutes then release remaining using quick release. Remove lid.
6. Add vanilla and heavy cream. Stir well and serve.

Nutritional Value (Amount per Serving):

- Calories 276
- Fat 10.9 g
- Carbohydrates 39.2 g
- Sugar 0.5 g
- Protein 5 g
- Cholesterol 21 mg

Chocolate Nut Spread

Preparation Time: 10 minutes
Cooking Time: 10 minutes
Serve: 4

Ingredients:

- 1/4 cup unsweetened cocoa powder
- 1/4 tsp nutmeg
- 1 tsp vanilla
- 1/4 cup coconut oil
- 1 tsp liquid stevia
- 1/4 cup coconut cream
- 3 tbsp walnuts
- 1 cup almonds

Directions:

1. Add walnut and almonds into the food processor and process until smooth.
2. Add oil and process for 1 minute. Transfer to the bowl and stir in vanilla, nutmeg, and liquid stevia.
3. Add coconut cream into the instant pot and set the pot on sauté mode.
4. Add almond mixture and cocoa powder and stir well and cook for 5 minutes.
5. Pour into the container and store it in the refrigerator for 30 minutes.
6. Serve and enjoy.

Nutritional Value (Amount per Serving):

- Calories 342
- Fat 33.3 g
- Carbohydrates 9.6 g
- Sugar 1.8 g
- Protein 7.8 g
- Cholesterol 0 mg

Conclusion

The recipes in Vegetarian Dash Diet Cookbook for Beginners will guide you in details so that you can make vegetable dishes without thinking too much and this cookbook will also help save your money and time. Uncover the delicious world of vegetarian and kickstart your new lifestyle! It is not just for breakfast, and once you master these easy basic recipes you can use them in myriad other recipes.

Wait no more!

Go ahead to have these recipes in your hand right now to lose weight, increase energy, and lower blood pressure.

Printed by BoD in Norderstedt, Germany